# Sight-Reading
## for ROCK GUITARISTS

### by Michael Mueller

Recording Credits: Michael Mueller, Guitar

Cherry Lane Music Company
Educational Director/Project Supervisor: Susan Poliniak
Director of Publications: Mark Phillips

ISBN 1-57560-659-3

*Visit our website at www.cherrylane.com*

# TABLE OF CONTENTS

# INTRODUCTION

If there is one glaring problem among guitar players it's that most don't read music very well. The blame for our not having sight-reading skills ultimately falls on our own shoulders as musicians—there's nothing stopping us from seeking out the proper instruction and then seeing it through via dedicated practice. But most of us signed up for our first guitar lessons at the local music store and begged our teachers to show us the latest and greatest rock guitar riffs. If we were lucky enough to have teachers who *could* read, we often dismissed the opportunity to learn how to do so ourselves, seeking instead more immediate gratification because we wanted to impress our friends with stilted versions of "Stairway to Heaven" or "Enter Sandman."

If being a rock star is your only goal, then you don't *need* to be able to sight-read, since most rock stars don't anyway. However, if you want to improve your odds of making a living by playing the guitar, I can't think of a more fundamental skill.

This book contains reading exercises both with and without tablature. As this book is aimed primarily at *rock* guitarists, I can understand that many of you may wish to use the exercises just to improve your tablature reading skills. If, however, you bought this book with the goal of learning how to sight-read melodies in standard notation, then you should try to avoid using the tablature altogether.

Now, go set up that music stand, find your metronome, and let's get started.

# ABOUT THE AUTHOR

Michael Mueller is the Managing Editor of *Guitar One* magazine. He authored *Guitar Techniques* and the *Hal Leonard Rock Guitar Method*, and co-authored *Scale Chord Relationships* and *Play Piano Today* (books 1 and 2) for the Hal Leonard Corporation. He holds an A.A.S. degree in Occupational Music from Milwaukee Area Technical College, where he studied guitar under Jack Grassel.

# HOW DO YOU BECOME A GREAT SIGHT-READER? PRACTICE!

The only way to become a proficient sight-reader is to sight-read—a lot! Be aware that the term "sight-read" implies certain rules about your practice. For one, you should work with a metronome and stay in rhythm. If you make a mistake, don't go back to correct it—keep moving. After all, if you make a mistake while playing live, the band doesn't stop so you can fix it. *Maintain the rhythm!* Also, when you practice sight-reading, you should not play the same piece twice in one sitting. After you've played it once, it's no longer sight-reading.

This book teaches you how to read single-note lines in treble clef only, but there is so much more to reading music: double stops, chords, different clefs, advanced dynamics and articulations, and more. Working through the rhythm lessons here can give you a solid foundation in the skill of sight-reading melodies. All it takes is 5–10 minutes a day of dedicated practice and, before you know it, you'll be able to sight-read. Consistency is essential.

# HOW TO USE THE CD

The included CD contains audio examples for many of the exercises found in this book. Try to play each of the exercises just once along with the CD. If what you're playing sounds exactly like the recording, then you're playing it correctly. But even if you're not, play each exercise *only once* and then move on to the next. Remember—if you practice the exercises repeatedly along with the CD until you can play them correctly, you're no longer sight-reading.

By the way, the audio examples were recorded with a Gibson Les Paul Custom and a 1983 Fender Squier Stratocaster through a Line 6 POD Pro into Ableton Live via an M-Audio Fast Track interface.

TRACK 01

Note: Track 1 contains tuning pitches.

# Chapter 1

# THE BASICS OF STANDARD NOTATION AND RHYTHM

## Standard Notation Basics

In music, different instruments have different ranges. Therefore, there are several different clefs to accommodate these differences. Guitar music is generally written in the *treble clef,* often referred to as the *G clef* due to the fact that one of the loops wraps around the staff line upon which the G note sits.

The staff itself consists of five horizontal lines and the four spaces between them. The pitch of a note is determined by its location on the staff. In the treble clef, the lines represent, from bottom to top, the notes E–G–B–D–F. The spaces in between represent, also from bottom to top, the notes F–A–C–E. You can remember these note locations using the mnemonics "Every Good Boy Does Fine" for the lines and "FACE" for the spaces.

Treble Clef

E    F    G    A    B    C    D    E    F

## Rhythm Basics

This book focuses on two fundamental elements of music: melody and rhythm. When first learning to read standard music notation, most guitarists focus on melody—that is, playing the right pitches. Although both components are crucial to making music, rhythm is perhaps a pinch more important in rock music. Picture this: You're playing in your rock band, and you play a wrong note. Amidst the din of the drums, keyboard, bass, and vocals, much of your audience may not notice your minor clam. Now, replay the scene: This time, you play the right note, but you play it one beat after everyone else. Depending on what's going on with the rest of the band—and particularly if that happens to be not very much, or even nothing at all—the entire audience may notice it.

The first key to playing rhythm correctly is to know and understand *time signatures.* Comprised of two numbers stacked one on top of the other, the time signature appears towards the beginning of the staff. The top number indicates how many beats appear within a measure (or bar) of music, and the bottom number indicates the type of note that represents one beat. The most common time signature in rock music is 4/4 (almost all of the exercises in this book are in 4/4). This means that there are four beats in each measure (top number), and a quarter note (bottom number) represents each beat on the page. Another common time signature is 3/4 (three quarter notes per measure). Now, you may be asking yourself "What's a quarter note?"

Think of a quarter note as the basic unit of measurement—it lasts for one beat in any time signature in which the bottom number is "4." A half note is the duration of two quarter notes. A whole note is equivalent to four quarter note beats; in other words, it lasts through an entire measure of 4/4. A half note, as you may have noticed, has exactly half the duration of a whole note.

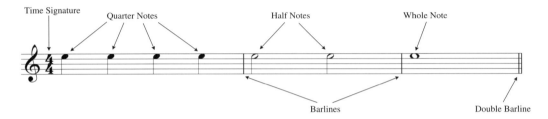

You may have also noticed the *barlines*. A single barline (such as the one between the quarter notes and the half notes in the music above) separates one measure of music from another. A double barline (like the one after the whole note) indicates the end of a section of music or an entire song.

But most music isn't made up of continuous notes—there are also periods of *rest*, or silence where one shouldn't play. To indicate these periods, there are symbols that are the rest equivalents to note values, such as quarter rests, half rests, and whole rests. They indicate that you should refrain from playing for the duration indicated.

Here's a short rhythm exercise. Set a metronome to 80 beats per minute (abbreviated as BPM from here on out). Tap your foot along with the metronome to the quarter note count of "1–2–3–4" and clap out the rhythm notated below. Once you're comfortable with this, try to play it on your guitar using any string. Clapping or tapping out a rhythm, by the way, is a great technique when you first approach *any* piece of music that looks a little tricky.

TRACK 02

Chapter

# THE NOTES IN OPEN POSITION

## A Note Primer

There are seven letters used to represent notes: A–B–C–D–E–F–G. These seven letter names repeat in order throughout the range of the guitar. One full "set" of notes that spans one full array of seven letters is called an *octave*.

Notes can be raised or lowered by one *half step* (same as one fret) as well, and this is indicated by ♭ or ♯ after a note name (or on the staff right before a note). The flat symbol (♭) indicates that the note is to be played one half step lower than normal (for example, E♭), and the sharp symbol (♯) indicates that the note is to be played one half step higher than normal (for example, C♯). Between the letter names and the *accidentals* (another name for flat and sharp symbols), there are actually 12 notes in each octave, each separated by a half step.

With this in mind, the real work now begins with the notes in *open position*, or those that can be played on the open strings or by fingering any of the first four frets. In open position, the index finger of the fretting hand fingers all notes on the 1st fret, the middle finger frets all notes on the 2nd fret, the ring finger frets all notes on the 3rd fret, and the pinky frets all notes on the 4th fret.

You can refer to the diagram below as you work through the open-position exercises. Note that the top line represents the high E (1st) string on the guitar, the string closest to the floor as you're playing the instrument.

```
E ┌─ F ──┬─ F♯/G♭ ─┬─ G ─┬─ G♯/A♭ ─┐
B ├─ C ──┼─ C♯/D♭ ─┼─ D ─┼─ D♯/E♭ ─┤
G ├─ G♯/A♭ ─┼─ A ──┼─ A♯/B♭ ─┼─ B ──┤
D ├─ D♯/E♭ ─┼─ E ──┼─ F ──┼─ F♯/G♭ ─┤
A ├─ A♯/B♭ ─┼─ B ──┼─ C ──┼─ C♯/D♭ ─┤
E └─ F ──┴─ F♯/G♭ ─┴─ G ─┴─ G♯/A♭ ─┘
```

You may have noticed that some of the notes on the fretboard have two names (e.g., F♯/G♭). These are called *enharmonic equivalents*, which is to say that they are the same pitch, but can be named in more than one way. Usually, you'll see the sharp versions of notes in sharp keys and flat versions of notes in flat keys (don't worry—you'll learn about keys in the next chapter).

# The High E and B Strings

The 1st or high E string when played open sounds an E note. On the staff, the E note occupies the top space (between the top two lines).

Now, place the index finger of your fretting hand on the 1st fret of the 1st string and play that note. This is an F, and it occupies the top line of the staff.

Next, place your ring finger on the 3rd fret of the 1st string and play that note. This is a G, and it occupies the space above the top line of the staff.

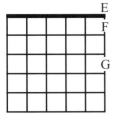

The 2nd or B string played open sounds a B, which sits on the middle line of the staff.

Place the index finger of your fretting hand on the 1st fret of the 2nd string and play. This C occupies the second space from the top of the staff.

Next, place your ring finger on the 3rd fret of the 2nd string and play. This D occupies the second line from the top of the staff.

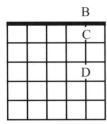

Here's the first of the many sight-reading exercises in this book; this one uses the three rhythmic values of the last chapter (whole note, half note, and quarter note) and their corresponding rest values, plus the six notes that were just covered. Before you dig in, be sure to set your metronome to a tempo of 60 BPM or another tempo that's more comfortable to you. Each click of the metronome represents one quarter note, so a full measure or a whole note will last for four metronome clicks.

**TRACK 03**

# The G and D Strings

The 3rd or G string played open sounds a G, which sits on the 2nd line from the bottom of the staff.

Have you noticed that you've now learned *two* G notes? These are in different octaves, but they're essentially the same note. Play the G on the 3rd fret of the 1st string and then the open G string. Do they sound similar? They should— they're the same note, in a sense. You'll see this concept repeat itself throughout the fretboard.

Now, place your middle finger on the 2nd fret of the 3rd string and play. This A occupies the second space from the bottom of the staff.

Next, place your pinky finger on the 4th fret of the 3rd string and play. This B note is the exact same pitch as the B of the open 2nd string. For the exercises in this chapter, you should play the B note on the open 2nd string.

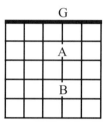

The 4th or D string played open sounds a D and occupies the space immediately below the bottom line of the staff.

Now, place your middle finger on the 2nd fret of the 4th string and play. This E note sits on the bottom line of the staff.

Next, place your ring finger on the 3rd fret of the 4th string and play. This F note occupies the bottom space of the staff.

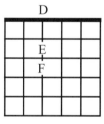

This next sight-reading exercise incorporates all of the notes covered so far (skip the B note on the 4th fret of the 3rd string for now). Again, set your metronome to 60 BPM or another tempo that's comfortable for you and play in strict time. Remember: Do not stop in the middle if you make a mistake. Keep going—*always maintain the rhythm.*

## The A and Low E Strings

Now, it's obvious that there are only so many lines and spaces on the staff, so how do you represent the notes that are too high or low to fall within its scope? The answer is through the use of *ledger lines*—small lines that sit above or below the standard music staff to effectively "expand" it. Just as on the staff lines, notes can fall either on or between ledger lines.

For instance, the 5th or A string played open sounds an A, which can be found on the second ledger line below the staff.

Next, place your middle finger on the 2nd fret of the 5th string and play. This B sits just under the first ledger line below the staff.

Now, place your ring finger on the 3rd fret of the 5th string and play. This C sits on the first ledger line below the staff.

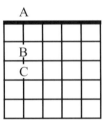

The 6th or low E string played open sounds an E, which occupies the space just below the third ledger line below the staff. By the way, it sounds two octaves lower than the open high E string.

Next, place your index finger on the 1st fret of the 6th string and play. This F note sits on the third ledger line below the staff.

Now, place your ring finger on the 3rd fret of the 6th string and play. This G note occupies the space just under the second ledger line below the staff.

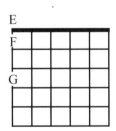

This next exercise uses notes from the 5th and 6th strings and then integrates notes from the other four strings. As before, set your metronome to 60 BPM or another tempo that's comfortable to you and play in strict time. Keep on going if you make a mistake.

**TRACK 05**

## A Little Sight-Reading Tip

The key to successful sight-reading is the ability to look one or two (or more) notes ahead of what your hands are playing at any given time. This is a skill that develops slowly and organically. As you progress, you'll be able to take in groups of notes or entire phrases at a single glance; the brain can become capable of processing an astonishing amount of information at once. As your comfort level increases, try to practice this skill. It will pay off greatly.

# Chapter 3

# TABLATURE AND KEY SIGNATURE BASICS

## Tablature Basics

If you've ever paged through rock or popular sheet music for guitar, you've probably noticed a staff below the standard notation staff. This is the *tablature staff*. Tablature (or *tab* for short) was originally developed centuries ago as a form of stringed-instrument notation.

The six lines on the tab staff represent the six strings of the guitar; the lowest line represents the low E string. A number on a line represents a fret location of a note that is to be played on that particular string. For example, a number "3" placed on the 2nd line from the top indicates the note on the 3rd fret of the 2nd string of the guitar (D). A "0" indicates that a string is to be played open. Here are a few examples.

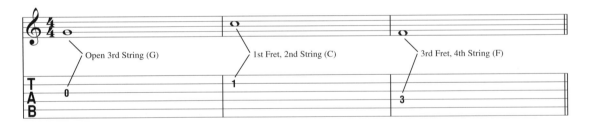

The strongest argument for using tab to read guitar music is that it provides valuable information as to the fret and string positions at which notes should be played. Many notes can be played in more than one location on the guitar. Remember the open 2nd string B, and how the same note can be played on the 4th fret of the 3rd string?

While tablature can provide string and fretboard position, there is no rhythmic element to the system. A small handful of sheet music publications have begun to attach rhythm stems, flags, and beams to tablature numbers to attempt to fill the void, but this is the rare exception and not the rule. Any good guitarist should be able to read standard notation and tablature pretty much simultaneously, much as any good pianist should be able to read the two staffs of standard piano notation at the same time.

Many guitarists use tablature to determine the proper fretting for a song and then get the rhythm information by listening to a recording of that song. This method is fine, but it won't help you if you need to play something on the fly or for which no recording exists. To be a competent guitarist, you should be able to read tab plus standard notation, as well as just standard notation by itself.

These next two exercises include notes in open position shown in both staves. Work through them as slowly as you need to, but get used to reading *both staves*. In the second exercise, watch out for the B note that can be played on the 2nd or the 3rd string!

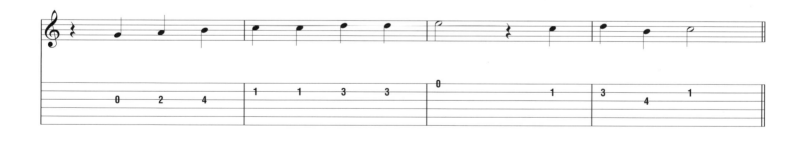

## Key Signature Basics

The *key signature* indicates the key in which a song is to be played. It is a set of sharp or flat symbols that appears on the standard notation staff immediately to the right of the treble clef. If a note is indicated as sharp or flat in a key signature, then it and every other note with the same letter name (for example, all of the Fs or all of the Bs) are to be played sharp or flat every time they appear in the song (there is an exception—more on that in a moment).

Here's what a key signature looks like. This one indicates that all Fs and Cs are to be played sharp.

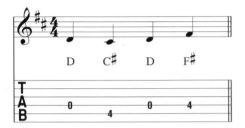

Flats and sharps can also be used by themselves right on the staff with notes, but they hold for only the measure in which they appear. So, for example, if you see a C with a sharp in front of it in the middle of a measure, and then see a C in the next measure without a sharp symbol, that first C is to be played sharp, but the one in the next measure is not.

An accidental can also be "cancelled" by a *natural* symbol (♮). For example, if a key signature calls for all Fs to be played sharp and you see an F with a natural symbol in front of it, you should play just an F—not an F♯. Just like sharps and flats, a natural symbol holds for only the measure in which it appears.

You may sometimes see a natural, sharp, or flat symbol in parentheses. These are called *courtesy accidentals*, and they're there to remind you that whatever accidentals occurred in the previous measure, things are back to "business as usual" according to the key signature. (It's also common to see courtesy accidentals without parentheses.)

With all of this talk of key signatures, you may be wondering what exactly a *key* is. A key, simply put, is a scale or group of notes on which a song is based. Generally, a key is named by the first note of its scale, and then the type of scale it is—for example, "C major." The C major scale consists of the seven notes counting up from C: C–D–E–F–G–A–B. In fact, you can find the scale of any key by beginning on the "key note" and counting up seven letter names, adding in whatever sharps and flats have been indicated by the signature. By the way, all of the exercises you've played so far have been in C major, and this key signature is indicated with nothing at all—no sharps or flats.

If this is all a bit confusing, don't worry—in the pages following, you'll do a lot of work with major keys. It will all seem very easy before long.

# READING IN OPEN POSITION

The next few chapters cover reading exercises that are specific to various key signatures. The ones in this chapter specifically involve the notes in open position.

## The Key of C Major

As was stated previously, the notes in the key of C major, which contains no sharps or flats, are C–D–E–F–G–A–B. But before moving forward to some reading exercises, here's a new rhythmic value to learn.

An *eighth note* has one half the rhythmic value of a quarter note. So, there are two eighth notes in the space of one quarter note, and eight eighth notes in one measure of 4/4. Eighth notes may appear on the staff in one of two ways: a lone eighth note as a quarter note with a small *flag* on the stem, or two or more eighth notes in succession connected by a *beam*.

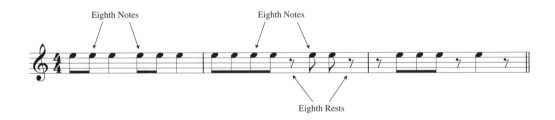

There are also *eighth rests* in the staff above. An eighth rest looks a little like an ornate numeral "7." Like an eighth note, an eighth rest has one half the rhythmic value of one quarter rest.

Whereas quarter notes can be counted "1–2–3–4," eighth notes divide a single beat in half and are therefore counted with the addition of the word "and": "1-and–2-and–3-and–4-and." Each of the preceding syllables has exactly the same duration—the "ands" go in between the quarter note clicks of your metronome. By the way, you'll often hear musicians refer to a phrase as beginning on the "and" of one (the second eighth note in the measure) or the "and" of four (the eighth eighth note in a measure of 4/4).

The following exercises are in the key of C major and include eighth notes. If you're having trouble, try counting "1-and–2-and–3-and–4-and" to the quarter note click of your metronome, set at 60 BPM or slower, if you need it.

**TRACK 08**

**TRACK 09**

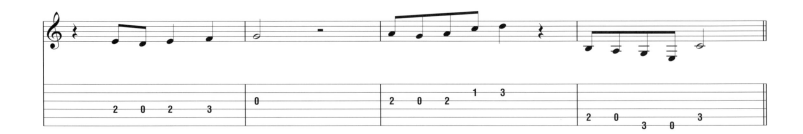

## The Key of G Major

The key of G major contains one sharp, F♯, and the notes G–A–B–C–D–E–F♯. The following exercises are in the key of G major, so each time you come across an F note on the staff, play F♯ (one fret above F). As always, use a metronome.

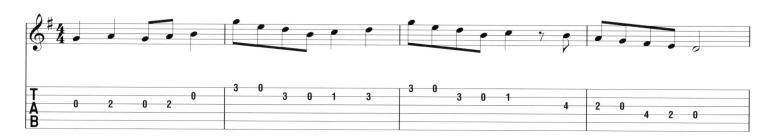

## The Key of F Major

The key of F major contains one flat, B♭, and the notes F–G–A–B♭–C–D–E. The following exercises are in the key of F major; each time you come across a B note, play B♭ (one fret below B).

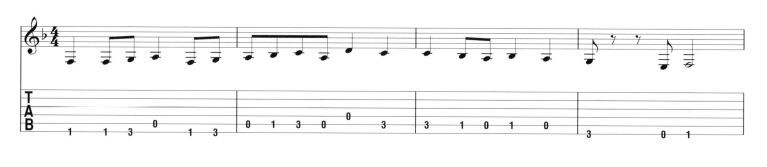

**TRACK 14**

# READING IN 2ND POSITION

## The Notes in 2nd Position

In 2nd position, your fretting hand's index finger frets the notes on the 2nd fret, your middle finger covers the 3rd fret, your ring finger grabs the notes on the 4th fret, and your pinky finger handles the notes on the 5th fret. No open strings are used in the 2nd position.

Here are the notes of 2nd position.

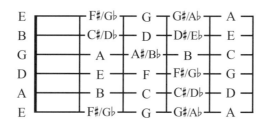

Take a look at the note on the 5th fret of the 1st string. This is an A, and it sits on the first ledger line *above* the staff.

Also, some of the notes now have additional tab locations. For example, the note on the 5th fret of the 3rd string is a C—the same pitch as the C on the 1st fret of the 2nd string. Play the C note at each of the above locations. They sound the same, right? On a typical electric guitar, this particular pitch occurs at *five* fretboard locations!

Try playing all of the notes in 2nd position—starting on the 6th string, going to the 1st string, and then working your way back—naming the notes aloud as you play them. This vocal exercise should help you to learn the locations of the notes on the fretboard quickly.

## The Key of D Major

The key of D major contains two sharps, F♯–C♯, and the notes D–E–F♯–G–A–B–C♯.

But before the exercises for this key, here's a new concept: *dotted notes*. When you see a small dot to the right of a *notehead* (the oval part of a note), it indicates that the note lasts for one and a half times its duration. For example, if a dot appears next to a quarter note, it lasts the length of one and a half quarter notes—the same as a quarter note plus an eighth note, or three eighth notes. If a dot appears next to a half note, it lasts for one and a half half notes—the same as a half note plus a quarter note, or three quarter notes.

Now, try playing the following D major reading exercises in 2nd position.

TRACK 15

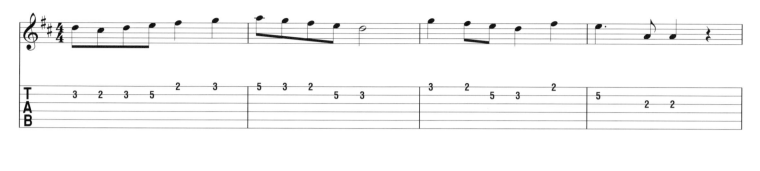

## The Key of A Major

The key of A major contains three sharps, F#–C#–G#, and the notes A–B–C#–D–E–F#–G#.

Play the following A major reading exercises in 2nd position. Notice in the second exercise (measure 6), however, that the note G# on the second line from the bottom of the staff does not occur between frets 2 and 5! You'll need to stretch either your index finger back to the 1st fret on the 3rd string, or your pinky finger out to the 6th fret on the 4th string to play this note.

**TRACK 18**

# Eighth Note Triplets

As you know, there are two eighth notes within the rhythmic space of one quarter note. If you divide the rhythmic space of a quarter note into *three* equal durations, however, you have an *eighth note triplet*. Count eighth note triplets in the following manner: "1-uh-let–2-uh-let–3-uh-let–4-uh-let."

Eighth Note Triplets

The following exercises are the most complex yet, with whole notes, half notes, quarter notes, eighth notes, and eighth note triplets as well as an occasional natural sign. The first exercise is in the key of A major and includes the tab staff. The second, however, is for the ambitious sight-reader—there is no tab on which to rely. But, as a reward for your hard work thus far, it is in the key of C major and should be played in open position.

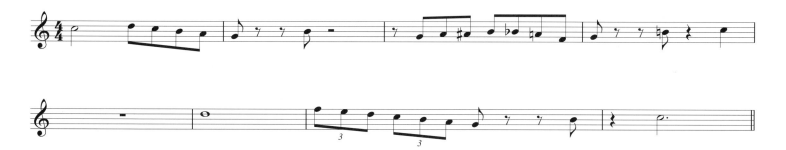

# Chapter 6

# READING IN 5TH POSITION

## The Notes in 5th Position

In 5th position, your index finger frets all of the notes on the 5th fret, your middle finger frets all of the notes on the 6th fret, your ring finger frets all of the notes on the 7th fret, and your pinky frets all of the notes on the 8th fret. Play the notes in second position, saying each note name aloud as you play it

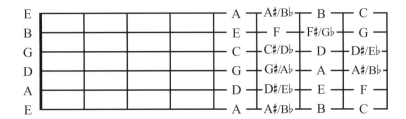

The space above the first ledger line above the staff holds the B note (1st string, 7th fret), and the note on the second ledger line above the staff is a C (1st string, 8th fret).

# The Key of B♭ Major

The key of B♭ major contains two flats, B♭–E♭, and the notes B♭–C–D–E♭–F–G–A. Play the following reading exercises in 5th position.

**TRACK 21**

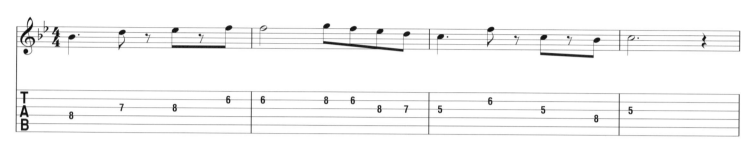

**TRACK 22**

# The Key of E♭ Major

The key of E♭ major contains three flats, B♭–E♭–A♭, and the notes E♭–F–G–A♭–B♭–C–D.

But before you try the reading exercises, here's a new notation concept. Sometimes, notes are held for a duration that crosses either a barline or the middle of a measure. In this case, as well as in certain others, a *tie* (an arc extending from one notehead to the next) is used to link the notes. When you see two notes tied together, play only the first note but let it ring for the summed duration of all of the notes that are tied together. For example, for an eighth note tied to a quarter note, you should play the eighth note and hold it for the duration of an eighth note plus a quarter note. Note that in tablature, usually only the first note of a tie is indicated by a number.

TRACK 23

Now, play the following E♭ major reading exercises in 5th position.

TRACK 24

# Chapter 7

## ARTICULATION TECHNIQUES

### Hammer-Ons

A *hammer-on* occurs when one plucks one note and then sounds the note that follows not by picking it as well, but by "hammering" another frethand finger onto a higher fret on that same string. In notation, this technique is indicated with a *slur* (an arc; it looks like a tie, so be careful!) connecting the two noteheads. For example, to execute the hammer-on in the first measure below, fret the D (5th string, 5th fret) with your left-hand index finger, play the note, and then, without removing your fretting finger from the string, forcefully fret the E (5th string, 7th fret) with your ring finger. Try playing through the full exercise—but don't forget to pay attention to the rhythmic values of the notes!

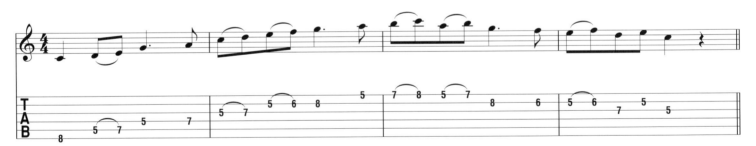

TRACK 26

# Pull-Offs

A pull-off, which is also indicated with a slur, is the opposite of a hammer-on. In order to execute the pull-off in the first measure below, fret the G (2nd string, 8th fret) with your pinky and the E behind it (2nd string, 5th fret) with your index finger, play the G, and then pull your pinky finger up and off the fretboard, allowing the E to ring. You may find it useful to pull down on the string with your pinky ever so slightly to help the second note to sound.

Hammer-ons and pull-offs are frequently used in succession in rock guitar. When this happens, a slur connects the first and last notes of the group. Remember to pluck only the first note!

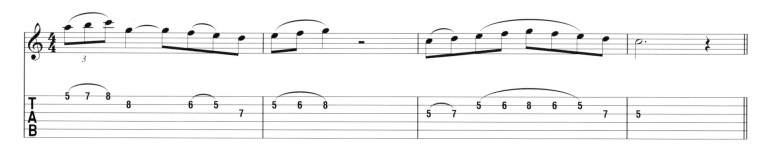

## Slides

Another popular technique in rock guitar is the *slide*. This technique involves playing one note and then sliding a fretting finger (usually the one with which you fretted the first note) either up or down the string to the fret location of a second note; you pluck only the first note. This technique is shown in notation with a diagonal line between notes plus a slur. Slides can occur in groups of more than two, just as hammer-ons and pull-offs.

TRACK 29

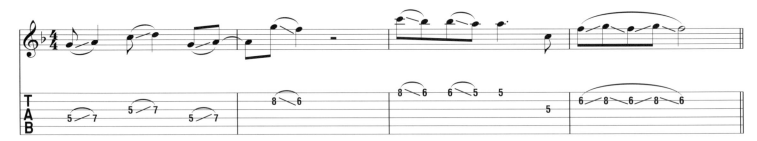

Sometimes, slides will be notated without starting or ending pitches. Generally, these indicate short slides to or from a note, but otherwise let context and good judgment be your guides.

## Bends

*Bends* are very common in rock guitar; just about any decent solo has notes that gradually change pitch due to bending. This technique involves fretting a note and then bending the string with the fretting finger (either pulling the string down towards the floor or pushing it upward towards the ceiling) to raise the pitch anywhere from a *quarter step* (equivalent to half a fret—very little pitch change at all) to, on rare occasions, two whole steps (equivalent to four frets!). The note is plucked before, during, or after the bend, depending on the notation. The most common bends are half steps and *whole steps* (equivalent to two frets, or two half steps).

In standard notation, a quarter step bend is indicated with just a very small arc, but otherwise a bend is indicated with what looks like an angled slur connecting two pitches. If a bend is to be performed in a specific rhythm, an angle connects the notes involved, as in the case of the half step bends below. If it is to occupy no real time in terms of rhythmic value, then the note from which it begins is indicated with a small notehead, as in the case of the whole step bends below. *Pre-bends* require that a note be bent before the string is plucked; these are indicated with a slur plus a small notehead in parentheses, as in the case of the one-and-one-half step bends below. All of these bends are indicated in tablature using curved arrows with numbers that indicate the number of steps ("1/2" for a half step bend, "1" for a whole step bend, etc.). Notice that for pre-bends, the arrow is straight, not curved.

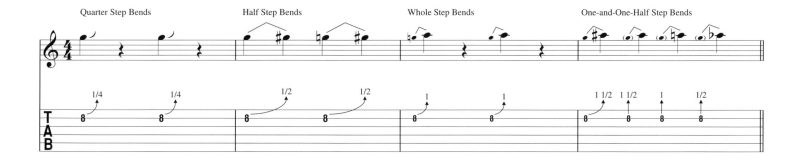

The reading exercise below is in 5th position and contains several standard bends that occur frequently in rock guitar music. Also, it is in a new key: A minor. "What," you say, "there are *minor* keys, too?" Yes, but don't fret. You'll read much more about minor keys in the next chapter.

Notice that in measure 4 there is a bend with a "return." This just indicates that the note is to be "unbent" or released back to its original pitch.

**TRACK 30**

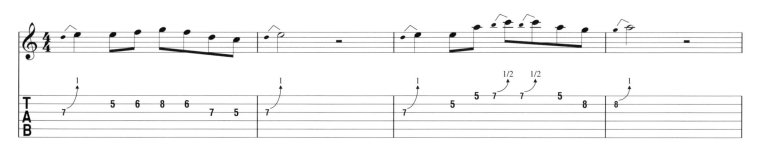

# Vibrato

*Vibrato* is a subtle, repeated pitch fluctuation that is caused by slightly and repeatedly bending a string in both directions (down towards the floor and up towards the ceiling) across the fretboard. Generally, you pull and then push the string back up again with a fretting finger. In both standard notation and tablature, vibrato is indicated with a bold, wavy line. The exercise below is almost the same as the previous one and contains vibrato on several longer notes. Listen for the differences. The speed and distance a given note is bent determine the extent of its vibrato.

**TRACK 31**

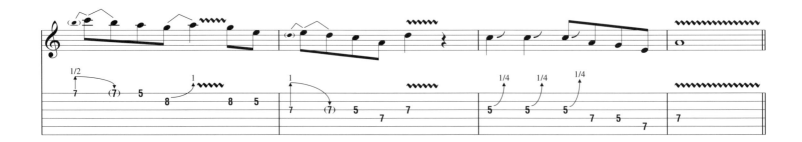

# Harmonics

*Harmonics* are those bell-like tones produced when a string is lightly fretted just over its fretwire and then played. The pitch of a *natural harmonic* (there are other kinds, but we'll cover only this one here) is notated on the staff with a diamond-shaped notehead; the tab indicates the string and fret where the note should be played. Harmonics most commonly occur on the 12th, 7th, and 5th frets, where they are easiest to produce clearly. Below are the natural harmonics on all six strings at these three fretboard locations.

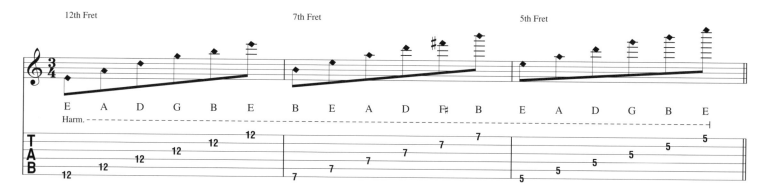

This next exercise requires a pretty fast position shift from the 12th-fret harmonics to the 5th-position melody. Play the harmonics with the ring finger of your fret hand; this can help to facilitate that move.

# Chapter 8

# READING IN 4TH POSITION

## The Notes in 4th Position

Since we've already covered the names of the notes in 2nd and 5th positions, you already know the notes in 4th position. For quick reference, however, here's a fretboard diagram as well as all of the notes and their tab locations on the staff. As before, play every note and say its name aloud as you go.

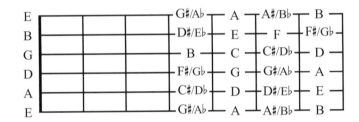

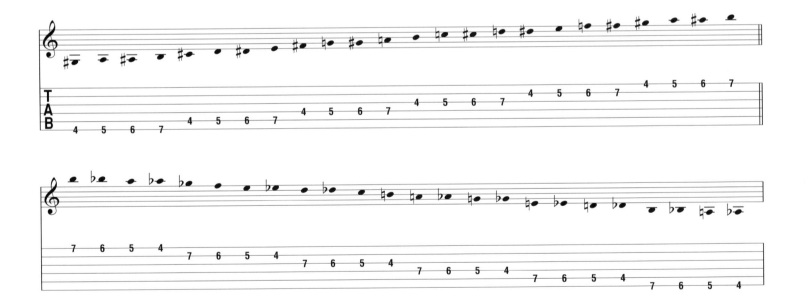

# Minor Keys

In the previous chapter, you played an exercise in the key of A minor, which contains the exact same notes as the key of C major. In fact, for every major key, there is a *relative minor* key that contains the same notes and key signature. It's easy to find the relative minor key of any major key: just fret the first note of the major key's scale (remember: it's the note that the key is named after, so in C major, it's C), and then count back three frets. For instance, if you count back three frets from a C, you get an A; the relative minor key of C major is A minor. Conversely, the *relative major* key of A minor is C major.

You learned several chapters ago how to list all of the notes of any major scale; it's just as easy to list the notes of a minor scale. Simply begin on the "key note" and count up seven letter names, adding in whatever sharps and flats have been indicated by the key signature. For instance, the notes of the A minor scale are A–B–C–D–E–F–G, and there are no sharps or flats since it shares a key signature with C major.

Now, you may be wondering why we even bother to make a distinction between C major and A minor (and any other related major and minor keys, for that matter) since they contain the same notes. Well, most songs in major just have a different "feel" than those in minor; many people say that major keys sound "happy" and minor keys sound "sad." Shifting the first note down three frets really does change things, especially when you throw chords into the mix. It can be a subtle distinction sometimes, but an obvious one once you're "keyed" into the difference and have played lots of music in both major and minor. For instance, if you're dealing with a song that has a C major/A minor key signature and the melody starts or ends on an A, it's a good bet that it's in A minor. If it starts and ends on C, it's probably in C major.

Here's a list of all of the major keys and their relative minor keys.

| | |
|---|---|
| C Major = A Minor | F Major = D Minor |
| G Major = E Minor | B♭ Major = G Minor |
| D Major = B Minor | E♭ Major = C Minor |
| A Major = F♯ Minor | A♭ Major = F Minor |
| E Major = C♯ Minor | D♭ Major = B♭ Minor |
| B Major = G♯ Minor | G♭ Major = E♭ Minor |
| F♯ Major = D♯ Minor | C♭ Major = A♭ Minor |
| C♯ Major = A♯ Minor | |

## The Key of E Major

The key of E major contains four sharps, F#–C#–G#–D#, and the notes E–F#–G#–A–B–C#–D#.

The first exercise below is in the key of E major (play it in 4th position), but the second is in its relative minor key, C# minor. Remember, the key signatures are identical, but in the second exercise, the C# note feels like "home." For an added challenge, the second exercise does not contain tablature!

**TRACK 34**

**TRACK 35**

# Sixteenth Notes

A 16th note is one half the duration of an eighth note, which means that there are four 16th notes in the space of one quarter note (or 16 16th notes in a measure of 4/4). The 16th note subdivisions are counted out loud as follows: "1-ee-and-uh–2-ee-and-uh–3-ee-and-uh–4-ee-and-uh." Each of the syllables has exactly the same 16th note duration. There are also 16th rests, which look like an eighth rest with an additional flag on top—a little like a numeral "7" with an extra top line.

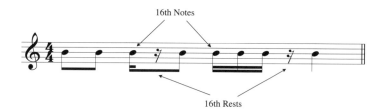

16th notes are often paired with eighth notes within the space of one beat. Here are some of the most common "combination" rhythms. Try tapping them on a tabletop to get a feel for them. Once you have these in your head, you can automatically "call them up" while playing; you won't have to think about them while you're sight-reading.

TRACK 36

Once you feel familiar with these rhythms, try this next exercise in E major.

TRACK 37

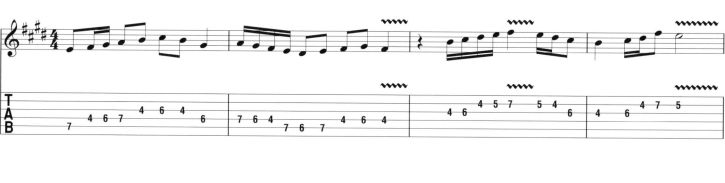

## The Key of B Major

The key of B major contains five sharps, F#–C#–G#–D#–A#, and the notes B–C#–D#–E–F#–G#–A#. Play the following exercise in 4th position.

**TRACK 38**

But wait—there's more! You know the dot—it can increase a note's length by one half of its original value. A dot can also be placed next to an eighth note. A dotted eighth note receives the rhythmic value of an eighth note plus one 16th note, or three 16th notes. The exercise below has several instances of a dotted eighth note followed by a 16th note to "complete" a quarter note beat.

**TRACK 39**

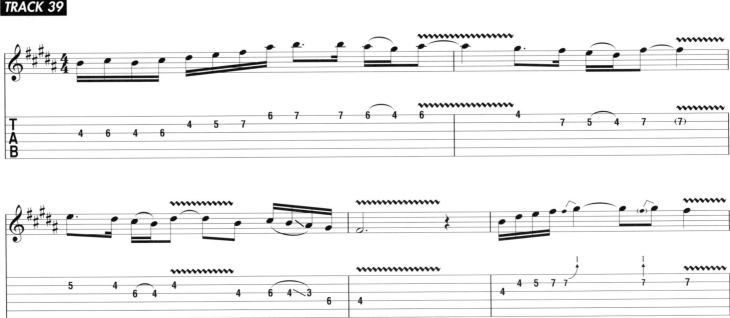

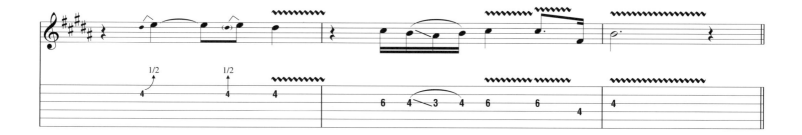

## Shuffle Rhythms

The *shuffle rhythm* is what gives jazz and blues its "swinging" feeling, and it puts the boogie in rock 'n' roll. The shuffle is a triplet-based rhythm, applied most frequently to eighth notes, in which pairs of eighth notes are played as if they were an eighth note triplet with the central note omitted.

You may hear musicians refer to music that is *straight* or *swung*—the difference is in how each beat is divided. In a straight rhythm (sometimes referred to as *straight eighths*), music is played as though each quarter note is made up of two eighth notes, as per usual. In a swung rhythm (sometimes referred to as a *shuffle rhythm* or *swung eighths*), you get the triplet feel that comes from treating each pair of eighth notes as though they're the first and last notes of a set of eighth note triplets. Notice that the notation is the same, except for a shuffle indication just above the staff.

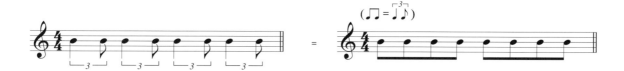

The end result of a swing or shuffle groove is a rhythmically propulsive "feel" that never fails to get folks' feet a-tapping along.

Listen to this example of straight eighths on the CD.

**TRACK 40**

Now, listen to the same example played in a shuffle rhythm, and notice again that the only difference in notation is the swing indication above the staff.

Try to mimic the difference in your playing. If you're not feeling particularly comfortable with the concept of shuffle rhythms, seek out recorded examples (most jazz and blues albums are laden with them) and play as many things in this rhythmic feel as you can in order to build up a bit of comfort with this ubiquitous groove.

The next exercise is a swinging boogie line in A major—without tab! Stretch your pinky to the 9th fret to grab that high C#.

# READING IN 8TH POSITION

## The Notes in 8th Position

In 8th position, your index finger frets all of the notes on the 8th fret, your middle finger frets all of the notes on the 9th fret, your ring finger frets all of the notes on the 10th fret, and your pinky grabs all of the notes on the 11th fret. Play through the notes in 8th position, saying each note name aloud as you go.

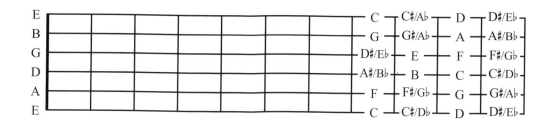

The space above the second ledger line above the staff is home to the D that is played on the 1st string at the 10th fret, and the D♯ (or E♭) that is played on the 1st string at the 11th fret sits on the third ledger line above the staff.

## The Key of A♭ Major

The key of A♭ major contains four flats, B♭–E♭–A♭–D♭, and the notes A♭–B♭–C–D♭–E♭–F–G. Play the following exercises in 8th position.

**TRACK 43**

**TRACK 44**

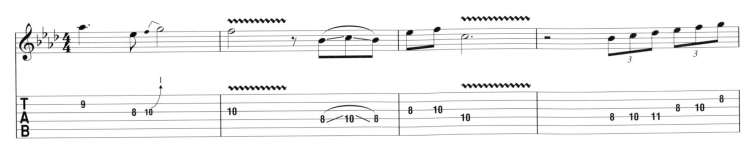

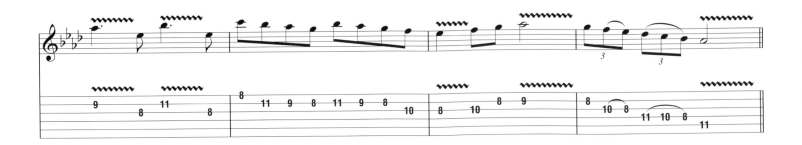

# Quarter Note Triplets

Whereas eighth note triplets are defined as three eighth notes occurring within the rhythmic space of one quarter note (or two eighth notes), quarter note triplets are defined as three quarter notes occurring within the rhythmic space of one half note (or two quarter notes).

Traditionally, musicians find quarter note triplets a bit tricky when they first attempt them. There's a little mental trick you can use to help you feel quarter note triplets when you're just getting started with the concept. While counting out two sets of eighth note triplets (six triplet notes), play only the first, third, and fifth notes out of the six as per the diagram below.

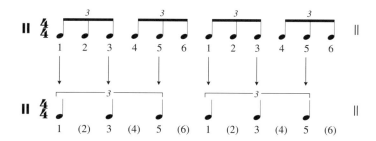

Try this quarter note triplet exercise on for size; it's in the key of G major and should be played in 2nd position.

**TRACK 45**

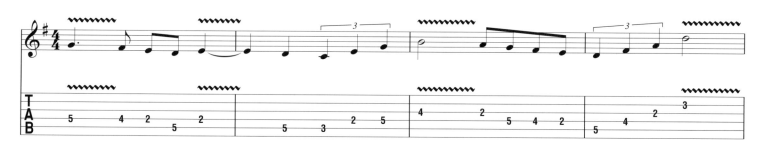

## The Key of D♭ Major

The key of D♭ major contains five flats, B♭–E♭–A♭–D♭–G♭, and the notes D♭–E♭–F–G♭–A♭–B♭–C. Play the following exercises in 8th position. The tab has been omitted from the second one for an extra challenge.

**TRACK 46**

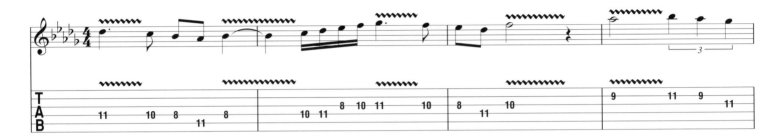

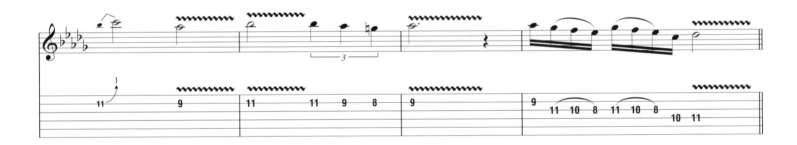

**TRACK 47**

# The Key of F♯ Major

The key of F♯ major contains six sharps, F♯–C♯–G♯–D♯–A♯–E♯, and the notes F♯–G♯–A♯–B–C♯–D♯–E♯. Play the following exercises in 8th position.

**TRACK 48**

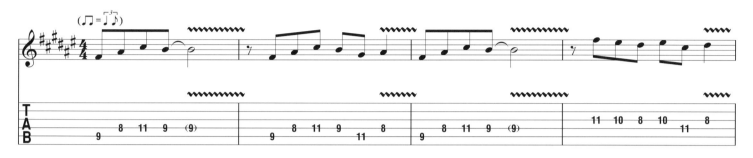

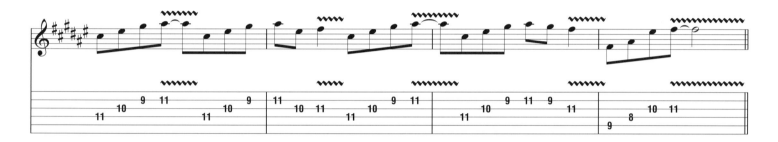

**TRACK 49**

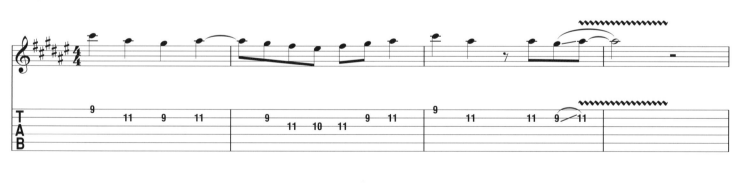

## The Key of G♭ Major

The key of G♭ major contains six flats, B♭–E♭–A♭–D♭–G♭–C♭, and the notes G♭–A♭–B♭–C♭–D♭–E♭–F.

Here, you have an example of enharmonically equivalent keys. F♯ major and G♭ major contain exactly the same pitches—they're just "labeled" differently. Play the following exercises in the key of G♭ major in 8th position.

**TRACK 50**

**TRACK 51**

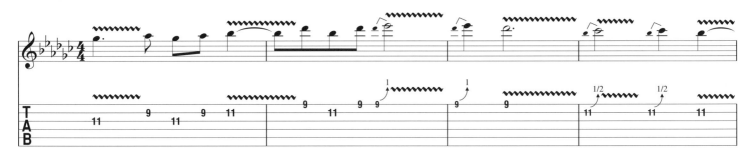

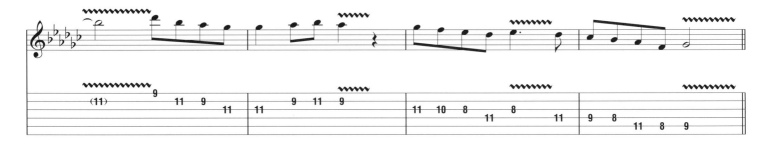

# The Key of C♯ Major

The next-to-last key is C♯ major, in which every note is sharp: C♯–D♯–E♯–F♯–G♯–A♯–B♯. This key is enharmonically equivalent to the key of D♭ major. It may at first appear that reading D♭ major is easier than reading C♯ major, as there are only five flats in the former as opposed to seven sharps in the latter. But think about it: If all of the notes are sharp, there isn't much to remember as you read. You just play *everything* sharp! Keeping that in mind, take a crack at the following exercises in the key of C♯ major in 8th position—but watch out for the accidentals!

**TRACK 52**

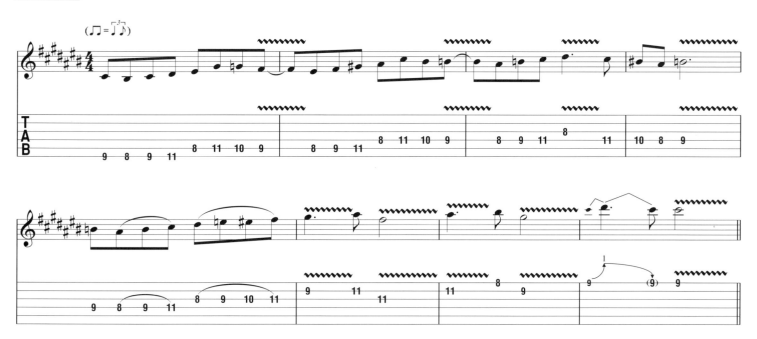

**TRACK 53**

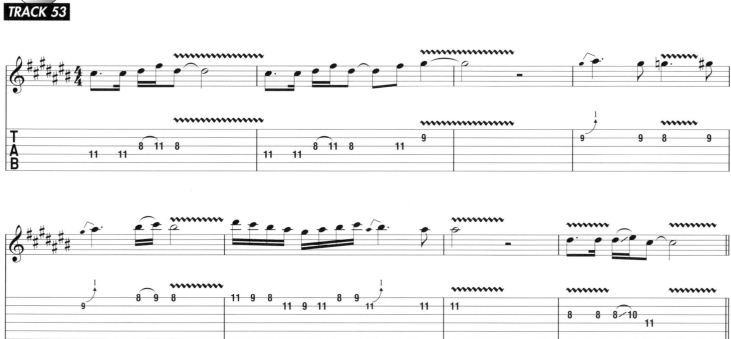

# The Key of C♭ Major

The final key is C♭ major, in which every note is flat: C♭–D♭–E♭–F♭–G♭–A♭–B♭. This key is enharmonically equivalent to the key of B major. Play the following exercises in the key of C♭ major in 8th position. Notice that you'll have to slide your index finger back a bit to catch the notes on the 7th fret!

**TRACK 54**

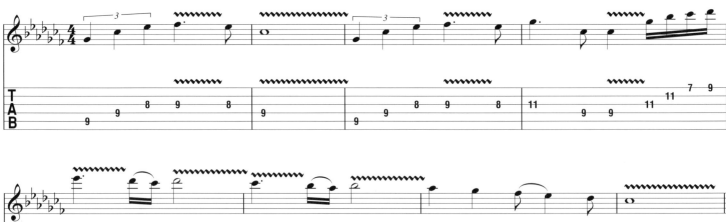

**TRACK 55**

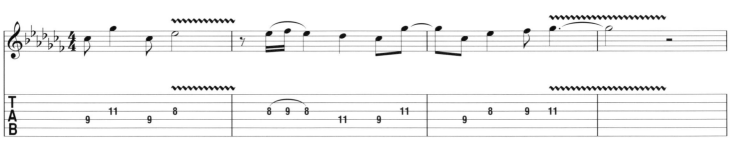

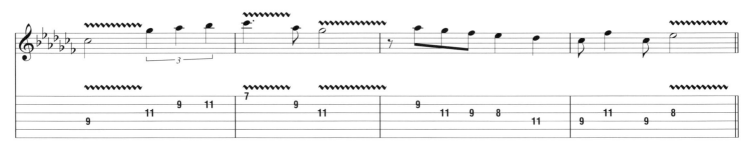

# Chapter 10

## READING EXERCISES

The rest of this book is comprised of reading exercises—a few with tablature, most without. Use a metronome for every exercise, and try to use the tablature only when you *really* need to find your way.

Always remember to check key signatures before playing through a new piece of music. A quick scan (when possible) to locate the highest and lowest notes in a piece can often be extremely helpful in determining its range and the most advantageous fingering position when no tablature is present.

Some of the exercises are particularly challenging, as they contain very little standard phrasings or melodic contours. You cannot necessarily rely on your ear to help you guess where the line will go next! Play them slowly if you need to, and take heart in knowing that if you can sight-read lines like this proficiently, you should be able to handle just about any melody without breaking a sweat! Later, when you've completed the work in this book, continue your sight-reading education on your own by practicing your new skills everyday (a mere ten minutes daily can help immeasurably), and be on the lookout for new and unfamiliar music to read. Good luck!

**TRACK 56**

**TRACK 57**

**TRACK 58**

**TRACK 59**

TRACK 60

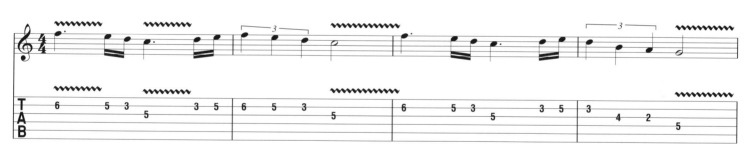

TRACK 61

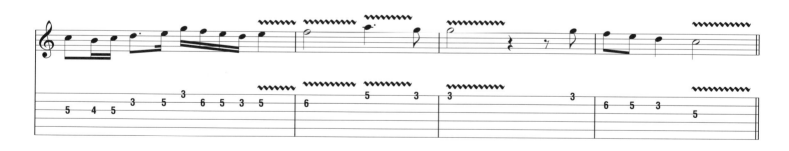

**TRACK 62**

**TRACK 63**

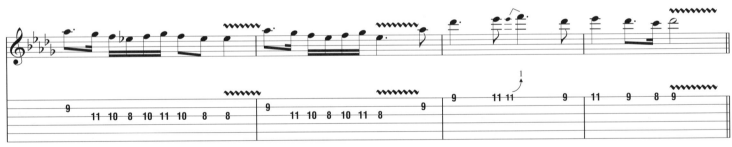

**TRACK 64**

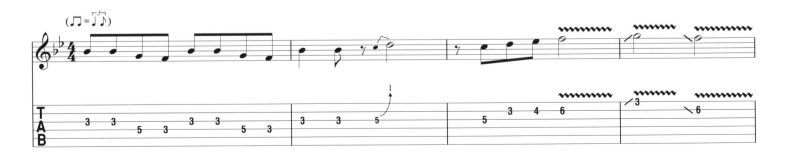

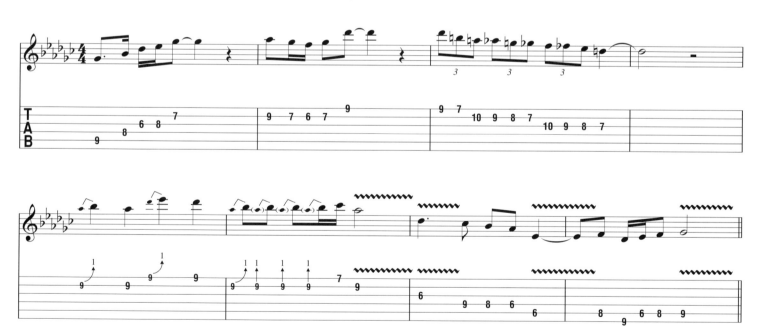

**TRACK 67**

**TRACK 68**

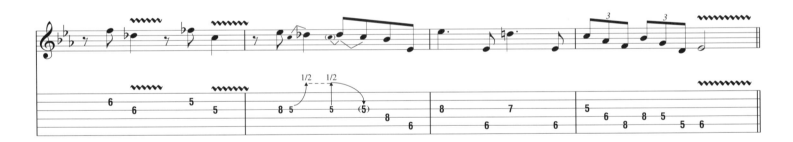

**TRACK 69**

Harm.

TRACK 70

TRACK 71

TRACK 72

TRACK 73

TRACK 74

TRACK 75

TRACK 76

TRACK 77

TRACK 78

TRACK 79

TRACK 80

TRACK 81

**TRACK 82**

**TRACK 83**

**TRACK 84**

**TRACK 85**

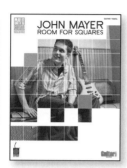

## CHERRY LANE MUSIC COMPANY

6 East 32nd Street, New York, NY 10016

*Quality in Printed Music*

**The Magazine You Can Play**

Visit the Guitar One web site at **www.guitarone.com**

### ACOUSTIC INSTRUMENTALISTS

*INCLUDES TAB*

Over 15 transcriptions from legendary artists such as Leo Kottke, John Fahey, Jorma Kaukonen, Chet Atkins, Adrian Legg, Jeff Beck, and more.

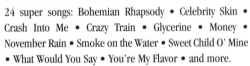

02500399  Play-It-Like-It-Is Guitar ............................$9.95

### THE BEST BASS LINES

24 super songs: Bohemian Rhapsody • Celebrity Skin • Crash Into Me • Crazy Train • Glycerine • Money • November Rain • Smoke on the Water • Sweet Child O' Mine • What Would You Say • You're My Flavor • and more.
02500311  Play-It-Like-It-Is Bass ............................$14.95

### BLUES TAB

*INCLUDES TAB*

14 songs: Boom Boom • Cold Shot • Hide Away • I Can't Quit You Baby • I'm Your Hoochie Coochie Man • In 2 Deep • It Hurts Me Too • Talk to Your Daughter • The Thrill Is Gone • and more.
02500410  Play-It-Like-It-Is Guitar............................$14.95

### CLASSIC ROCK TAB

*INCLUDES TAB*

15 rock hits: Cat Scratch Fever • Crazy Train • Day Tripper • Hey Joe • Hot Blooded • Start Me Up • We Will Rock You • You Really Got Me • and more.
02500408  Play-It-Like-It-Is Guitar............................$14.95

### MODERN ROCK TAB

*INCLUDES TAB*

15 of modern rock's best: Are You Gonna Go My Way • Denial • Hanging by a Moment • I Did It • My Hero • Nobody's Real • Rock the Party (Off the Hook) • Shock the Monkey • Slide • Spit It Out • and more.
02500409  Play-It-Like-It-Is Guitar ............................$14.95

### SIGNATURE SONGS

*INCLUDES TAB*

21 artists' trademark hits: Crazy Train (Ozzy Osbourne) • My Generation (The Who) • Smooth (Santana) • Sunshine of Your Love (Cream) • Walk This Way (Aerosmith) • Welcome to the Jungle (Guns N' Roses) • What Would You Say (Dave Matthews Band) • and more.
02500303  Play-It-Like-It-Is Guitar..........................$16.95

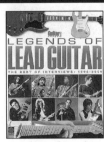

### BASS SECRETS

WHERE TODAY'S BASS STYLISTS GET TO THE BOTTOM LINE
*compiled by John Stix*
*Bass Secrets* brings together 48 columns highlighting specific topics – ranging from the technical to the philosophical – from masters such as Stu Hamm, Randy Coven, Tony Franklin and Billy Sheehan. They cover topics including tapping, walking bass lines, soloing, hand positions, harmonics and more. Clearly illustrated with musical examples.
02500100  ..........................................$12.95

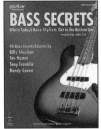

### CLASSICS ILLUSTRATED

WHERE BACH MEETS ROCK
*by Robert Phillips*
*Classics Illustrated* is designed to demonstrate for readers and players the links between rock and classical music. Each of the 30 columns from *Guitar* highlights one musical concept and provides clear examples in both styles of music. This cool book lets you study moving bass lines over stationary chords in the music of Bach and Guns N' Roses, learn the similarities between "Leyenda" and "Diary of a Madman," and much more!
02500101  ..........................................$9.95

### GUITAR SECRETS

*INCLUDES TAB*

WHERE ROCK'S GUITAR MASTERS SHARE THEIR TRICKS, TIPS & TECHNIQUES
*compiled by John Stix*
This unique and informative compilation features 42 columns culled from *Guitar* magazine. Readers will discover dozens of techniques and playing tips, and gain practical advice and words of wisdom from guitar masters.
02500099  ..........................................$10.95

### IN THE LISTENING ROOM

WHERE ARTISTS CRITIQUE THE MUSIC OF THEIR PEERS
*compiled by John Stix*
A compilation of 75 columns from *Guitar* magazine, *In the Listening Room* provides a unique opportunity for readers to hear major recording artists remark on the music of their peers. These artists were given no information about what they would hear, and their comments often tell as much about themselves as they do about the music they listened to. Includes candid critiques by music legends like Aerosmith, Jeff Beck, Jack Bruce, Dimebag Darrell, Buddy Guy, Kirk Hammett, Eric Johnson, John McLaughlin, Dave Navarro, Carlos Santana, Joe Satriani, Stevie Ray Vaughan, and many others.
02500097  ..........................................$14.95

Visit Cherry Lane online at **www.cherrylane.com**

### LEGENDS OF LEAD GUITAR

THE BEST OF INTERVIEWS: 1995-2000
This is a fascinating compilation of interviews with today's greatest guitarists! From deeply rooted blues giants to the most fearless pioneers, legendary players reveal how they achieve their extraordinary craft.
02500329  ..........................................$14.95

### LESSON LAB

This exceptional book/CD pack features more than 20 in-depth lessons. Tackle in detail a variety of pertinent music- and guitar-related subjects, such as scales, chords, theory, guitar technique, songwriting, and much more!
02500330  Book/CD Pack......................................$19.95

### NOISE & FEEDBACK

THE BEST OF 1995-2000: YOUR QUESTIONS ANSWERED
If you ever wanted to know about a specific guitar lick, trick, technique or effect, this book/CD pack is for you! It features over 70 lessons on composing • computer assistance • education and career advice • equipment • technique • terminology and notation • tunings • and more.
02500328  Book/CD Pack......................................$17.95

### OPEN EARS

A JOURNEY THROUGH LIFE WITH GUITAR IN HAND
*by Steve Morse*
In this collection of 50 *Guitar* magazine columns from the mid-'90s on, guitarist Steve Morse sets the story straight about what being a working musician *really* means. He deals out practical advice on: playing with the band, songwriting, recording and equipment, and more, through anecdotes of his hard-knock lessons learned.
02500333  ..........................................$10.95

### SPOTLIGHT ON STYLE

THE BEST OF 1995-2000: AN EXPLORER'S GUIDE TO GUITAR
This book and CD cover 18 of the world's most popular guitar styles, including: blues guitar • classical guitar • country guitar • funk guitar • jazz guitar • Latin guitar • metal • rockabilly and more!
02500320  Book/CD Pack......................................$19.95

### STUDIO CITY

PROFESSIONAL SESSION RECORDING FOR GUITARISTS
*by Carl Verheyen*
In this collection of colomns from Guitar Magazine, guitarists will learn how to: exercise studio etiquette and act professionally • acquire, assemble and set up gear for sessions • use the tricks of the trade to become a studio hero • get repeat call-backs • and more.
02500195  ..........................................$9.95